A Death on Skunk Street

"Only in poetry can pathos be reduced to near aphorismic density. Reading William S. Friday's "A Death on Skunk Street" shows us how. Friday's collection is a book of ghosts. In it, he gives us the bitter pill of life and sweetens it with touches of irony and sarcasm, allowing us into, and out of, the pain of the poet's world."

- Lois P. Jones

    Poetry Editor, Kyoto Journal

"A purposeful and uncompromisingly honest introspection of a quest for balance without all the usual artsy-fartsy pompous Kool-Aid political dogma bullshit that passes for poetry today. Good fucking job on this book."

- J.W. Gardner

    Author, 'In the Shadow of the Bomb'
    Creator/Producer, The Last Sunday

"I've been a fan of William S. Friday's poems for some time now and I'm thrilled to see this collection of highly personal, existential poems. Friday does not shy away from delving deep inside and allowing himself to bleed all over the page. This is what poetry SHOULD be, and I have no doubt that Bill will make a lasting impression with this highly intense work."

  - Julian Gallo
    Author, 'Breathe'

"Concise. Emotional. Personal. It's obvious that the thoughts and feeling expressed in Bill's poetry are deeply felt, and I admire anybody who can express themselves that way. It's good work."

  - Derrick Ferguson
    Author, The 'Dillon' Series

First Edition, May 2016

ISBN 978-0692701591

Printed in the United States of America

Ordering Information:
Quantity sales. Special discounts are
available on quantity purchases by
corporations, associations, and others.
For details, contact the publisher.

Hostile 17 Print

www.hostile17print.com

A Death on Skunk Street

Written By

William S. Friday

Hostile 17 Print

For Mary.

Her face is my home.
All the pride I take
in the earth beneath my feet.
The only reason I will stay.
They who wish a piece of me will come here,
or be from here.
They who want me to go, there's the door.
My one true love,
and no one will be closer to my heart than she.

- Grandpa. April 2016

For Daran, Benjamin, and Michael.

Blood of my blood.
Bone of my bone.
The imprint on my soul.
Because you are, I am still.

Thank You

To Derrick Ferguson and Julian Gallo, fellow
Citizen Journalists, and crafters of worlds with
your words...

Sarah Fader, fighter of every good fight... Joe
Gardner and Lois P. Jones, poets and welcoming
hosts of poets whose voices must be heard...
and Ra Avis, my editor and the teller of every
good story yet to be told. Thank you for your
wisdom in the preparation of this book. To each
of you, I offer my gratitude.

To Jessica Ceballos and Karineh Mahdessian, who
welcomed me into the uncountable number of poets
who call Los Angeles their home...

Conney Williams, whose words showed me that a man
can feel, and express those feelings through the
spoken word...

Alicia A. Young, who taught me that your home is always with you in the love of your children...

Don Kingfisher Campbell, who opened his classroom to me and trusted my voice with his students... and Professor Betty Dillon, the first person in this life who gave to me the belief that my words were worthy for this world.

To Alexis Cancio, Russell Almario, Joseph Mael, Jess Lourey, Tanya Chernov Smith, and Dean Walker. In an online world you have, by your very real examples, shown me it is safe to trust myself in the same ways you have trusted yourselves. The examples your lives have been to me have brought me to this place.

To The Last Sunday in Culver City, where I performed many of these poems in my first ever feature... Avenue 50 Studio in Highland Park, where I learned not to fear a circle of chairs...

Beast Crawl in Oakland, where I learned to trust strangers...

Beyond Baroque in Venice, where I learned to trust friends... and Los Angeles International Airport (LAX), where I learned to trust no one AND everyone, all at the same time. You were my laboratory in the creation of this book, and this path that is the rest of my life.

To Hostile 17 Print, my publisher... and Silver Star Lab, the Companion to my Doctor, nothing but good things ahead in all our futures.

WSF

Table of Contents

A Death on Skunk Street

Skunks lay low when it rains here
and possums stay off the slick streets,
restricting their business to
the tops of cinderblock walls
or inside dumpsters
under the pale blue cover of streetlights
and the shadow of kitchen windows' warmth.

Here the air around me smells of
wood-burning fireplaces
and fresh wet earth,
where the ocean gives up
its salt spray
on the sharp winds of night

Then comes the rolling sting
of pricking needle mist...
A gift sent from the
midnight leaden blanket of heaven.

It is on this street where

I turn my face upright to meet it,

and dream of what it will mean

when I die here.

8 Megapixels Deep

Drop the curtain of night
over the last burning
fire of creation.

Take the picture,
8 megapixels deep,
to let the world know
you were there.

Empty

Woke up empty this morning, wishing it was this
time yesterday.
Turned over and checked my phone to see if
anything had changed.
It hadn't.

Cleared my email
Rolled the other way,
closed my eyes, and wished myself to sleep.

It was better when I slept.
Dreaming.
Another bed... empty...
But at least I was there.

You and She

This life is easy.

Eat,

Sleep,

Fuck,

And make little yous and shes

who do the same after you,

and she...

...No,

wait.

This life is easy.

Feed the hungry,

Act tirelessly,

Give a fuck,

And make the world a little better

for those who come after you,

and she...

... No,

wait.

This life is easy.

Eat,

and feed the hungry.

Sleep,

and act tirelessly.

Fuck,

and give a fuck.

and make little yous and shes

who do the same for those who come after you,

and she

Sunday Scatological

I'd like to blame society,

... because, *shit*.

I'd like to blame sobriety,

but that's supposed to fix it.

I'd like to blame my life

... though it's never been bad.

I'd like to blame my ex-wife

(but the divorce isn't final)

I'd like to blame the entitled, tattooed,

... pimple-necked, twenty-something, hipster...

wannabe...

taking up the whole goddamned handicapped table

next to me at Starbucks

... not ordering a drink...

and using their free Wi-Fi

to share Neko Case on his cellphone with me,

against my will.

But he's just a symptom.
(and Facebook)

I'd like to blame Obama or Bush.
I'd like to blame Clinton,
... either or both.
I'd like to blame sound bites,
and memes and shit.

Maybe there's a reason to fight,
but that's not it,
because it's easier to just blame me
... or Facebook.

(Yeah
... fuck Facebook)

An Audience of Captives

I used to preach,

to an audience of captives in stiff-backed
chairs.

Theater seats that rose in rows from the pulpit
to the heavens,

thirteen in all.

I would speak,

mostly to the empties,

from the Gospels and the Book of Acts,

... because they move the way people move.

... smell the way people smell.

And humanity wasn't given a free pass.

The Moment After That

It starts with that feeling
between and behind
your open eyes...

the one that whispers,
"It's okay... shut them...
just for one second...
go ahead... let it go."

And it is then that you know.
The next moment
of your life
... will be spent
pressing down on the brake pedal...
or you will spend
the moment after that...

dying.

A Freudian Story

I have three
photographic obsessions...

the full moon,
the beach,
and dirty streets.

I take pictures of them
with my phone,

8 megapixels at a time...

more than
I take pictures of anything
else in the world

... and of sunsets,
but only at the beach...

If you lumped them all together,

they tell a Freudian story.

One that goes like this...

I'm cold and far off.

I'm dirty and hard,

and the only beauty

I have left

is fading

into dark.

Details

It's okay,
I completely understand.

You want all of me...
just not who I am.

You admire all that's made me the man I've
become,

you just can't embrace
the details.

These Memories Which Remain

I remember being cold, in the fog of another
school year. The field, east of the playground,
was soaked with the dew of leaden heaven, and my
thin flannel was the right weight for a forecast
that was proved wrong in the dark skies of ice
and water above.
I walked,
shivering like only a skinny child can. No meat
on my bird bones to carry with it
the warmth of the fireplace at breakfast.

This would be my only memory from that day, lost
among ten-thousand others. There would be no
connection from one bright experience of
childhood to another, and another. Only that I
was cold
and underdressed. That the sky was battleship
gray in the middle of morning. And that I do not
recall what came next.

Life at that age, 10... maybe 11... was a series
of disconnected events.

Cold hands, stinging throughout an entire
baseball practice in March.
That almost-daily fog that soaked and chilled.
The sucker punch from a Straight-A earning, mop-
haired bully. And every name of the 8th grade
graduation processional, memorized.

Along with the wish that, one day, everything
would just make sense. That, sometime soon, all
would turn to good
for a kid whose only recurring dream was to be a
ghost.

And that these memories which remain
would not be forever.

Breath on Windowpanes

Before I got there
it was gone
All the words that
went with every feeling of my heart

Pain
not acute enough to notice
except when accompanied by the will to
give in.
... Give up ...
my pursuit of happiness
in the way that turns colors to
chalk beneath December rain,
and breath on windowpanes
into wishes
that will not fade until
the coming of spring.

Once Burnts

Quitting is easier.
You just stop.

Of course the consequences
of concerns
laid bare
Hurts,
and the scars that accompany

Twice shys from
more-than-once burnts,

And the dreams
The visions of your heart
that come
if only to explain

what it means

Holes

Sometimes
we
fill
holes
in
our
lives,

with

deeper

holes.

Today

There are days
when I think I have
lived long enough.

Days after birthdays,
and when holidays have
passed for the year.
Personal days of remembrance...
... anniversaries
and deaths.
Days of finality after celebration
or mourning.
Days that follow
the emptying of my soul.
Days I can't remember
why I've hung on
for so long.

Today.

What Happens When

Is this what happens when...

...you don't grow up before you play grown-up?
Straining for the toys and cookies of the grown-
up world, before you learn to fly, and fall, and
land, and stand on your own feet. Wanting to
fuck before you learn how to figure things out,
like love, or loss, or who you even are when you
look yourself in your own mirror.
And settling for the first smile that tells you
she'll stay,
if only you play by her rules,
because that's what grown-ups do.

Is this what happens when...

... no one shows you how to be a man?
Tripping over yourself trying to please, before
you have the first clue of what pleases. Knowing
what you want, without learning how to have it.
Needing what you've not been shown. Showing that

there is not one good thing you can't do without,

because you've satisfied yourself with shit.

And accepting the words of strangers,

because it's easier than having convictions of

your own.

Is this what happens when...

A Lament for Children and Trolls

The world is fucked. Look at your TV.
Look at your city.
Look at your country.

Now look in your mirror.
Aspartame in Jell-O
kills children's brain cells.
Suicide bombs
turn children's brains into Jell-O.
Online trolls tell you who you can
and cannot weep for.

I choose to weep for the children.
I choose to weep for the trolls.

Because ... obviously,
neither one knows any better.

Talisman

Some people wear talismans,
bracelets,
a necklace,
charms that dangle for the
pious crowd.

The talismans I wear...
Scars.
A reminder,
ransom invisible to all,
Seen only by those I allow,

Healers, a lover,
an undertaker in silent prayer.

My life is a talisman unseen,
a reminder,
like a bad tattoo
I allow others to wear.

The Straw Man

I think I've said my peace
now that the past
isn't changing for
the future.

You're going to do what

you're going to do.

I say hi every day

when you don't,

so you don't think I'm some kind

of bad man.

You're going to do what

you're going to do.

I am the opposite of

a good man...

I am the straw man

you made up to describe me.

Netflix

Bad timing, and loneliness,
and impatience, and fear.

All that has, or ever will, drive me.

Move ahead when I should stop.

Want, and want wrongly,
when I should just smile politely
and walk the other way.

Keep your friends close, and out of your bed.
And do not fall in love.
Not with the wrong person.
Not with the right person.
Not at all.

That's what drinking or working,
or Netflix is for.

Double Tap

Drink till you fall asleep.

Wake up and drink,

till you pass out.   Repeat.

Double scotch.

Double tap to the head.

Just to make sure

your soul is dead.

Look at the pictures.

Read the posts.

Whisper "fuck you"

to the ghosts.

So you didn't move on

at the fresh light of a new dawn,

upon the same old world,

silent for once.

Bright morning seen through

undeserving eyes.

Red and clenched against

the light of lies.

I thought I'd changed.

The Apology

I've been a shitty friend to a lot of you
and while I had my reasons,
I never had excuses.
I wish I'd been a better friend to most of you
or with some,
maybe just not known you at all.

That would have made life so much easier
... and most likely better,
at least for you.

Because whatever puny light my time in your life
brought
it would have been better if I'd left you in the
dark

Until somebody with a torch showed up
and lit your path
the way you deserved.

I'm Sorry

(Serial-One)

I say "I'm sorry" almost every time I stop long
enough to take it all in. A breath held deep,
and released slow. A long pull and swallow of a
cold, bitter beer. A glance that lingers in the
wrong direction. Every one an unfortunate
reminder of a broken something that can never be
set right, like a bone to be mended. Only to be
lived with, limped on. The pain, dull and almost
forgotten, a reminder.

In the Distant Shimmer

(Serial-Two)

Happiness is an illusion. We are told it can be found like water we are convinced exists in the distant shimmer of a mirage. One step, one lunge, one gulp of hot sand meant to slake the very thirst that was created by the illusion itself. Self-perpetuating. Self-fulfilling. Self-defeating. It kills as it gives life. Slowly, and with the surety of a lover's skilled hands. Convincing us that the way things are, is the way things should be. Even if we die in the process.

Purged

(Serial-Three)

I've been asked if I will ever write 'light', as
if the only emotion I have within me is 'dark'.
When that happens, I usually shrug. Not the
literal kind, with shoulders that move, and a
face like an open-mic comic delivering a
punchline. But an internal shrug that says, "You
wouldn't understand". These words of mine, in
their form and ordered on the page, are not an
extension of all that is within me, but an
expression of all that must be purged *out of me*.

The First Time in Thirty Years

There is
nothing harder than the
first month of something new.

First month of
Sobriety,
First month of
Celibacy,
First month of
paying your own bills for the
first time in thirty years.

First time you
were the only voice
inside your own head.

Whispers

Brains on the bathroom floor.

...Gloating

Consciousness above me.

... Floating

Despair at life unlived,

Responsibility relieved,

Bucket made of bone,

... a sieve...

Whispers of all doubt,

believed.

Sex Before Coffee

Sex before coffee.

Intimacy.

Naked in the morning.

Unashamed.

No fear

of wits being slow,

of words being wrong,

of harsh light telling truths

the shroud of night was

kind enough to cover.

Changing Things

My crushing defeats have never been
followed by victories,
only off-seasons of regret
and forgetfulness.

Waiting for the next spring,
and with it,
the insane hope of things changing
without changing things.

Ones and Zeroes

Time does not exist here.
There is a canvas of black letters,
afloat on a sea of pale pixels.

No ink.
No paper.

Only ones and zeroes,
taking the shape of dreams in the night.

No victims.
No heroes.

Just atoms that spark in electric flight.

The Dark Road Called Forward

[My world is lately upside-down.

Its only direction is the road before me,

and it is called, Forward.]

I have a past. We all do.

Mine is dark behind me,

and strewn with the debris

of unchangeable regret.

The burnt and mangled wreckage

of unsuspecting lives,

forfeit to the fog-wet highway,

taken too lightly.

Captured only in digital reminders

of the worst ending,

never imagined,

and what must have been

the better times before.

Times of lies rightly told,

and fears suppressed long enough to enjoy the

promise of surroundings that would fade away,

locked safe inside grief's scrapbook.

The open road, at night,

looks like life.

There is only what's in front of you,

insufficiently lit.

Just enough light to aim yourself, hurtling,

into more dark.

Behind you, there is nothing on which to dwell.

A last stop, last road sign, last lane change.

Or anything more

than the shadows of what might be gaining on you.

And in the distance, there are the cities,

distant, shining. Waking dreams, miles away

and full of the hope you foolishly still hold

onto, silent, in your heart.

Silent, because you know ,

while they were once beautiful, they are now

just the out-loud promises

you weren't meant to keep.

Mystical, glowing,

still drawing you

like a vision of your own clever words.

But up close, jagged, and beyond forgiveness.

A blue neon cement-scape of lives crumbled,

and nothing but dirt in the details.

So you accept only what you can see

in the light right before you.

You trust only that the destination ahead

is there as you've been told,

and that it waits for you.

You let all there is, shining in the distance,

go.

And you stay on the dark road called Forward.

Older and Frailer

I avoid thinking about my childhood
unless someone asks me to tell them
why I am the way I am,
... and then I'm forced to...

Or I lie.

And usually,
when I talk about the distant past ...

I spend that time remembering my dad
whose influence always finds
its way to the surface
of my thoughts
the quickest

He would yell
when he got angry,
mutter when he knew he was wrong,

and condemn

when warning me against things

that could lead to harm

but as he got older and frailer,

with age and a failing heart,

he also would

own up to his yelling,

muttering,

condemning ways and speak

with genuine contrition.

Until the last night I saw him alive

and I knew that he

loved me more on that night

than on any day

which had preceded it.

Coffee and Fortune Cookies

The universe is made of
coffee and fortune cookies,
Each one vital to the
existence of dreams,

...and neither the least bit
important
to any
but
the dreamers.

John Stephen Akhwari

I can't keep up with my own life,
let alone the lives of those around me...
... the lives of those who love me
and
God forbid...
of those I love.

Without meaning to,
my life has become the image that
haunted me in my wide-eyed post-adolescence
... of the Tanzanian marathoner,
John Stephen Akhwari,
who finished last in Mexico City in 1968.

Yeah...
just YouTube it.

The point is,
I want to grab onto life...

hold on for all I'm barely-worth...

... or run,

with endurance

and the speed

not just to finish

but to win.

Yet on days like this,

and most others,

it is all I can do to look at life like a

bandaged,

limping man...

... sweat-drenched and bloody...

shuffling in the dark towards the finish of a

race,

long over,

but not for himself,

who,

when asked why he did not quit a race

long-lost

said,

"My country did not send me five-thousand miles

to start the race.

My country sent me five-thousand miles

to finish the race."

And so,

I look up

into the near-empty stadium

... and to a victor's stand

long since abandoned by those with medals won,

and put one more foot in front of one more other.

This race almost done.

Ockham

The simplest answer

... usually...

is the right one.

(Thanks, razor-boy.)

Of all the

possible answers

to life's

dramatic questions,

The simplest never

includes the heart,

because the heart

has been

cut

out.

Waver

I waver
between imagined
happy endings,
and realized
disappointments,

Fearing
my unreadiness
for joy.

Sunday into Monday

It all collapsed at once.

Everything I had staked my future on had fallen

in on itself

And as I sat in my room, late Sunday into Monday

... alone..

with the TV on

and the space heater blowing up at me from the

floor...

I took long pulls on my second PBR

and typed,

Because there was nothing left to do.

I Drink Coffee

I drink coffee in the morning for the same reason
I drink whisky at night.

To cope,

to move on,
to survive.

I know they will
both, ultimately, kill me.

One slower, one faster, together a lot faster.
But
I know not having them will kill me, too.

Even slower still.

I Am Fucked No More

Epiphany in my time of greatest need,
that the shit on which I feed no longer satisfies
my empty beggars gut
as it once did.

I am whole within myself,

and no sorry-ass opinion of my well-chronicled
condition
matters now or in the future,
as it once did
... like before...

I'm telling all
from now on,

... broken
... gone

I am fucked no more.

Guarantee of time is a cruel lie,

a hate crime against the stupid and the

desperate...

...against me...

... against yourself.

There is now and there is now,

yesterday is dead,

tomorrow deader,

move or be consumed,

buried and exhumed

and killed again

... like before...

I'm holding nothing back

from now on.

... broken gone

I am fucked no more.

To see my end as a beginning,

like the blind see darkness clearer in the gray,

never once did...

... till today.

No peace, no tears, no closure,

no release from guilt or shame,

only what is built on bones that stand

and do not crumble

... like before...

I'm letting go

from now on.

... broken gone,

I am fucked no more.

Story done and over, but unfinished,

most or more than that

left unsaid,

as it should be,

till accounts are closed,

till I'm dead,

Till then... unsatisfied.

My fulfillment never closer,

never clearer,

one day said,

Victory won

from now on,

broken, gone...

I am fucked no more.

Three Weeks Till

I sniffled in the drip from
another morning of
almost-fall allergies... and
caught the taste of
coffee on my tongue... the
sun rises and sets in the
wrong place now...
hangs in the sky like a
torch, not a candle...
burns sepia, not gold... it's
still three weeks till the
end of summer... and
nothing feels farther away than the
promises of June.

The Heart of a Child

The heart of a child is never lost.

It can be anything but that.

It can be hidden beneath a fort made of blankets,

... impenetrable against the bitter cold of

encroaching adulthood.

It can inhabit the melt of marshmallows in

steaming cups of cocoa,

... becoming at once sticky sweet,

and imperceptibly smooth as sunlight,

reflecting off icicles, dripping at dawn.

The heart of a child is never lost.

It can be everything but that.

It can be found in grown men's laughter,

after touchdowns are scored...

in games they never played.

It can build itself a home in the midst of ruin,

...creating solid walls of faith out of the

crumbles of hope,

because love was always its foundation.

The heart of a child is never lost.
It is born
and again reborn.
It is as new as it is old,
... suckled in whispered nurture,
tender as it is strong.
It can be easily crushed or fortified,
in the simplicity of the spoken word,
... or the silent eyes of a mother's first
blessing.

The heart of a child is never lost.
It is all things to all people.
It is universally understood because its message
is simple,
using only small words inside short sentences,
so those older and wiser should not be confused.

Therefore,
it teaches those who should be teachers by now,
exposing such foolishness

quicker than a funhouse mirror on Halloween.

The heart of a child is never lost.

It is eternal.

And because it is without beginning or end,

it has never been constrained by time or space or

lines on a map to limit its message to those who,

for just one moment in eternity,

may have stopped listening.

And without which the message falls on deaf ears,

forever.

The Next Time

My childhood is the nightlight
of my waning years.
My dad died,
on the front porch of my childhood home,
at the age of 68.
His dog at his side.
Only God could tell you what he,
and the dog,
went through in that moment...
together,
like they spent most days of his retirement.

My mom still worked,
so she was not there when it all went down.
His final heart attack,
with Harry,
their next door neighbor,
finding him long after it was too late.
And Jo-Jo,

his little girl,

the Sheltie who kept him company.

Things we learn so late.

The hug. The smile and nod.

The dismissal of anger

when anger's escalation feels so much more

natural.

And the acceptance of the flaws of history,

in the things that can never change.

Because the past dies before we do,

yet we hold onto it tighter than we do our own

departed loves.

Three days before his passing on the porch,

I had my last dismissal,

in a dinner and a game

with the man whose whole existence would shape my

own.

Weakened by years and a failing heart,

he was now not the man of my youth,

but merely the container.

A shell of clear glass,

incapable of concealing anything,

especially the truth.

He was almost dead that night,

but in him I saw only life.

We said goodnight,

not in any sort of dramatic understanding of what

was to come,

but in the knowing way two people

of the same DNA hug,

then smile and nod,

expecting nothing more than to do it all again,

the next time.

Except the next time never came.

Muth Labben

Today is for counting my wasted yesterdays,
each one neatly lined up.
... Row, on dusty row.
Every year the same...

Today is for remembering your unborn tomorrows,
and the time I sit, because walking is too slow
There is no blame...

Today is for pretending to make sense of the past
From a life ended, with nothing to show
when I speak your name...

Today is for thinking that memories last,
but all they do is fade,
until they go...
Like every unfinished song to be sung
about the death
of a son.

In Words

Long ago, I learned to take 'no' for an answer.
In words.
And more when words aren't spoken,
and the absence of a 'yes'
whispers louder.

Break Even

Airborne highs
followed by
subterranean lows,
before that long climb
back towards
break even.

I really like
break even.

Regrets

I don't want to regret my regrets,
but enjoy them to the full...
The way a teenager enjoys the
back seat of a car at
eleven-forty-two pm
on a Friday night in September.

I'm pretty sure I love you
and no one else,
but I won't say it out loud or in print
until the day I can say it to your face,
when our lips and
tongues melt together
and nothing can tear us apart.

Just like the kids in that back seat felt
At eleven-forty-two pm...
... joined together,
neither being the other's first,

but believing with all they could know that

they would be each other's

last.

The Gnats I Kill

The music doesn't drown the certain tones of
those who speak because they know it all...
... I can hear them, I just don't want to...
and maybe my problem is,
they really do know it all,
and maybe I should be listening.

I don't listen well with others anymore...
the gnats I kill
between the fruit bowl and the trash can
pay a more absorbent attention than I do...

The chatter and the superficial geniality
in these encounters is suffocating...
but the only other option is the silence of
isolation...
yet it's the isolation that terrifies me more.

Is there any turning back?

Pacific Ocean

Three grand a month to
survive on my own
in a world where people go
bankrupt with millions...
Fear of the unknown
keeps me prisoner
in this well-lit rented home...
where the Pacific Ocean
is my oldest neighbor.

No better way to fall than to leap...
Land in a heap...
Can't remember the dreams when I sleep...
Wake up and let go
of the things I can't keep...

When I know there will always be me...

I'm just a poor man in a bad situation...

depending on more

than just the kindness of strangers...

family and acquaintances...

I made a mistake... not in moving on...

but in looking back...

and depending on the undependable

for the things they did not have

to give.

Golden

A place to live,

quiet and warm.

A dog,

big and loyal.

And a woman,

golden,

right and true,

who will love me

as much

as she loves the dog.

Three Heartbeats in Eternity

I spoke to a friend today,

much longer than I had the right to,

and learned that it was okay to just be.

I whined like a goddamned infant child,

and found a place to lay my head.

... And for what seemed like

three heartbeats in eternity,

I saw things as they really were.

I spoke to a friend today,

not as long as I would have liked to,

but guilt held onto me.

I felt like a thief,

shoving goodness into pockets full of shit.

I felt worse, then better by the end.

And for what seemed like

three heartbeats in eternity,

I didn't want to die.

And I kissed my fingers toward heaven.

The Preacher

"If I haven't made you sad, mad, or
glad," the preacher said,

"I haven't
done my job."

Life, preach.

Patient Son

I have lived here for 54 years, 2 months, 29
days, 19 hours, and 45 minutes, as of the moment
I started writing this.

With my thumbs, on my phone, in the aircraft-
hangar-sized United Airlines Cargo hub at LAX.

It has been a day, and now a night, of discovery,
of self-inspection,
of learning one final lesson about my time served
in this concrete shithole with the pretty name,
prettier ocean,
and prettiest promises never delivered to a
patient son.

I will find my inheritance, and claim it.
Just not here.

Sorry, dad.

Stand-up Man

I've made terrible mistakes
but possibly none greater than the
selling of myself
short.

When it comes to my
true value... to others...
one more nice guy
finishing last,
the world will not miss.

But one more stand-up man?

Fucking legend.

In the General Flow of All Good Things

The water rose and I almost drowned
over and again,
in so many ways,
unforeseen

It rose and receded,
and with each ingress
and egress,
I grew less aware of the strength that had
replaced my weakness

Then it was,
... at just the right time...
that I saw what had become of my position,
and my place
in the general flow
of all good things.

There was mud in my pants,

and I may have shit myself a time or two in the

process,

but I was standing ,

And hard as it was to move,

I moved.

One thick step after another.

Remembrance Day

The day my life began, I was already seventeen-
thousand, one-hundred and seventy days old. And
about one hour.

But what an hour.

I wasn't ready for her, but she was ready for me.
She was brown, if brown could be its own shade of
pastel.
Built like bull wire and tenderness in equal
measure, beneath a newborn exterior.

Mine, and more than my redemption.
Today is her day.

The eighth celebration of her life that we, the
ones who are graced by her, remember her with.
She is a normal eight-year-old girl. She loves
dolls and hockey, mac and cheese and Brussel

sprouts, Shel Silverstein, and Bob's Burgers.
She is loved, thank God, by her peers and her
elders.

And she, thank God, loves her peers and her
elders just the same.

And today, because there is love in this world
that would not have existed had she not entered
it, I write this.

For me. For her family. For her. Because one
day, she will read this, as she has already read
my poetry. And she will know that this is who
she is to us.

She is the daughter of my daughter.
She is the heart of my heart.

And this day will forever be her birthday. The
eighth so far. The remembrance day of when my
life began.
And hers.

Chasing

I've grown
tired
of chasing
dreams.

Dreams
will now
be chasing
me.

Feet for the Calluses

To trade this

now

for another

because parts of

now

make me sad,

to sever an arm

for the birthmark, or

feet for the calluses,

and deny my senses

for a life of fewer lessons,

curse my eyes

for the glasses

or my mouth

for the soap

that washed it out.

To not have held

the entirety of love

against my chest, then

carried it on feet

that have withstood

the weight of imperfection

but continued forward.

And trade the scars

that gave me beauty

in the infinite tomorrow

for an empty past

of losses unremembered,

is a cowardice

for fools.

Lucky Seat

I thought about moving from this seat
and from the glare of the afternoon sun
as it closed my eyes in a squint
against my reflection
in the laptop screen.

I thought about moving from this seat
and from the sting of the setting sun
as it burned itself three layers deep
into the skin
of my red right arm.

I thought about moving from this seat
and from the warmth of all good things
that had not felt this right
for so long
to have its way with me.

But I have written six poems in this seat

over the last two days

and I will be damned

if I'm going to do anything

to fuck this up today.

A Soft Place to Die

I am deeply, irretrievably, forever in love.
I just don't know with *whom*.
My heart is a lying monster, on the edge of
mayhem, ready to kill or be killed over something
as simple as the wounds in its heart.

There is an amalgam, a composite of tender
strands, to make this monster heart bleed like
fingers wrapped in dental floss, or enfold with
its entire rough body the wincing pain of the
paper cut that drives the soul to rage...

Set off by the smallest of things, and seen as
the biggest of fools for it...

And whether rage or passionate lust be the
signifier of what lies deep, deeper inside the
monster, it is only love, seeking love, which
gives the beast a soft place to die.

Tin Awnings

A lost weekend
looking out at the rain...
three lights on in the whole place...

The grey sky at dusk,
the computer on my lap,
and football on TV.

Not a one of them has inspiration for me
but in the silence of muted commercials
there is a sound,
from tin awnings across a row of balconies
out my back door,

Thick fat drops of words forming
one story above pavement,

One story after another.

Je Suis Zombie

I wish I wrote with a pad and pencil,

like the poets

who gargle with scotch

and espresso,

wrapped in causes like flags to be burned in,

camera-ready protests,

Fixing the world one

endless march of

rotting corpses

at a time.

Insensate herd,

well-meaning as

children selling cookies door-to-door,

while the enemy marches,

and believes... does not matter what.

Masses moving forward

in silence and darkness,

where good corpses

fear to tread.

Of Time and Inclination

It is,

finally,

all open before me...

The past,

and the future,

the same...

I can see my mom and my dad, and my great-grand-
kids,

as if nothing separates them...

The generations of those who share more than my

name...

beyond the DNA...

... deeper than the stories that show us only as

individuals on unrelated paths...

To the world,

we are no more

than the backside of a tapestry on public

display...

Unremarkable,

and only seen as such by those who pass by,

without regard for more than they can take in at

a single glance...

Without benefit of time and inclination to wait

for the reveal of the interwoven glory that is

the richness of the front side...

To them,

we are random threads...

Patternless...

Hidden from impatient eyes...

But to all,

from now on,

with one simple turn of the cloth...

Beauty for those who see.

End-Stage Living

Today I feel old.

My body reads like an accident report...

... chronically-sprained right wrist,

... back spasms,

... intermittently self-dislocating

ankles,

All from just living,

nothing catastrophic...

Only life lived at half-speed...

Yet for all the

dents and dings that mark

this future corpse,

I still don't look half bad...

... and maybe that's my problem.

I think I'm fucking up

by not dying from

end-stage living...

Roadmap(s)

There are reasons

I didn't release more than half the poems in my

catalog

before they were published...

I didn't want anyone reading the roadmap of my

past...

not anyone...

not even those who deserved to know

... it was private...

in this case so private that no one person should

have the clearance to know it all...

just a page here, a page there, like code...

never to be made public

until the folds of the map are made flat...

and they may never...

but I can show off some of those spread-out

pages...

then pass the rest down to a trusted someone,

yet unchosen...

who, though they didn't know...

won't take a shit in their pants

when they read what it was I could not say.

To Recapture My Humanity

I sit penned in, like a singular head of cattle.

Cement and wood and stucco form my enclosure,

and the white of clouds

foreground the blue of open sky,

not yet awash with the pastels of

another setting sun.

Until I hear

...as if for the first time, the wind,

in the sound of a lover's wincing pleasure,

between rough slats of painted pine behind my

head.

It is here that I sit and sip my morning coffee,

and try, for just this moment,

to recapture my humanity.

And in these words,

succeed.

About the Author

Fictionary. 8 Megapixel Artist. Bloody Awful Poet. William S. Friday is a bender of words, voice, and stuff.

A one-time Citizen Journalist, Bill became a poet out of necessity. Previously published online and in print, <u>A Death on Skunk Street</u> is his first solo project. He lives near the Pacific Ocean in the town of Redondo Beach, California.

13261322R00062